MW00700736

For Mike—
To a very
Kind and Wonderful
Mom—
With Warmest
Regards
Thanks!

2010

40's Wax Lips & 50's

White Bucks

LOOKING BACK AT WHAT WE DID

By Dennis Adler

STOOP ID Publications LLC

LOOKING BACK AT WHAT WE DID
IN THE 40's AND 50's

WAX LIPS AND WHITE BUCKS
copyright © 2009 by Dennis Adler

ISBN 13: 978-0-9824573-0-6
ISBN 10: 0-9824573-0-8
Printed in Korea

STOOP   ID   Publications LLC

This book is dedicated to my family, immediate and extended, especially the memory of my mother, Hilma, and my dog Sean.

Love, Dennis

Dennis Adler

1952

Special "thank you's" go to Don Callen of Faith Books
and Clyde Van Cleve of Van CLeve Graphic Design for their kind,
patient and generous assistance in bringing this publication to reality.
Thank you also to Bettina Miller of Reminisce magazine
and the people at Readers' Digest magazine for their enthusiasm
and thoughtful support. The persistent kindness and encouragement
of my friend and neighbor Paget Engen, of Pengen Consulting
cannot be forgotten. In addition, my gratitude to Mike Thaler
for his past and continued support of my creative efforts.
And of couse, "thank you" to all of my family and friends.
It is the kindness and support of others
that makes one's work meaningful.

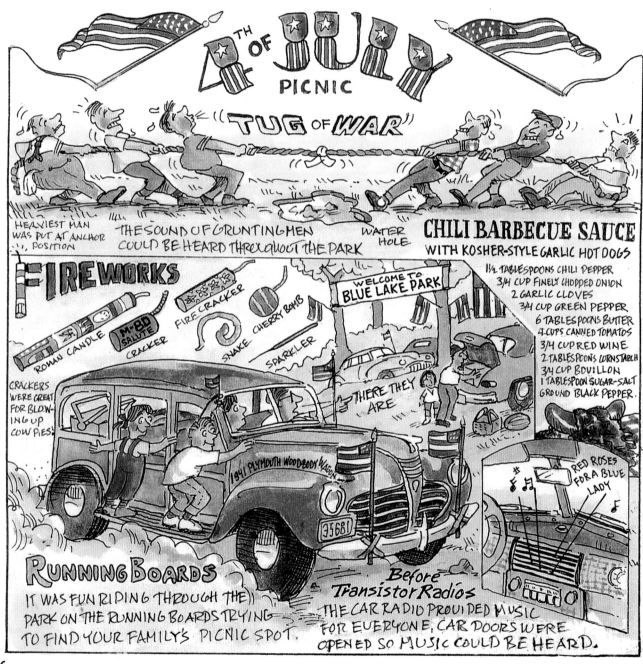

4TH OF JULY PICNIC

TUG of WAR

HEAVIEST MAN WAS PUT AT ANCHOR POSITION

THE SOUND OF GRUNTING MEN COULD BE HEARD THROUGHOUT THE PARK

WATER HOLE

CHILI BARBECUE SAUCE
WITH KOSHER-STYLE GARLIC HOT DOGS

1½ TABLESPOONS CHILI PEPPER
3/4 CUP FINELY CHOPPED ONION
2 GARLIC CLOVES
3/4 CUP GREEN PEPPER
6 TABLESPOONS BUTTER
4 CUPS CANNED TOMATOS
3/4 CUP RED WINE
2 TABLESPOONS CORNSTARCH
3/4 CUP BOUILLON
1 TABLESPOON SUGAR-SALT
GROUND BLACK PEPPER.

FIREWORKS

ROMAN CANDLE
M-80 SALUTE
FIRE CRACKER
CRACKER
SNAKE
CHERRY BOMB
SPARKLER

CRACKERS WERE GREAT FOR BLOWING UP COW PIES!

WELCOME TO BLUE LAKE PARK

THERE THEY ARE

1941 PLYMOUTH WOOD-BODY WAGON

35681

RED ROSES FOR A BLUE LADY

RUNNING BOARDS

IT WAS FUN RIDING THROUGH THE PARK ON THE RUNNING BOARDS TRYING TO FIND YOUR FAMILY'S PICNIC SPOT.

Before Transistor Radios

THE CAR RADIO PROVIDED MUSIC FOR EVERYONE. CAR DOORS WERE OPENED SO MUSIC COULD BE HEARD.

FLATTENING PENNIES

THE SANTA FE SUPER CHIEF TRAVELED DAILY BETWEEN CHICAGO AND LOS ANGELES

PENNIES WERE PLACED ON THE RAIL. THE WEIGHT OF THE TRAIN FLATTEND THE PENNIES TO A BIG ROUND SHAPE. STREET CAR RAILS WERE ALSO USED

PENNIES

SantaFe — Ride great trains through a great country 1951 SERVING THE WEST & SOUTHWEST

PEDAL PUSHERS HUNG BELOW THE KNEE

GIRLS PEDAL PUSHER PANTS

PENNY LOAFERS WERE A CASUAL SLIP-ON SHOE.

SHINY PENNIES FIT IN HERE MEANT GOOD LUCK.

COLOR BROWN

USED ORIGINALLY FOR BICYCLE RIDING

PEDAL PUSHERS AND PENNY LOAFERS

ROOT BEER SUCKER
WHITE ROPE HANDLE

PEZ
CANDY
SPRING ACTION DISPENSER

ORANGE SHERBET — TAB
VANILLA
WOODEN SPOON
ICE

DIXIE CUP ICE CREAM
SPOON LEFT A WOOD AFTER TASTE

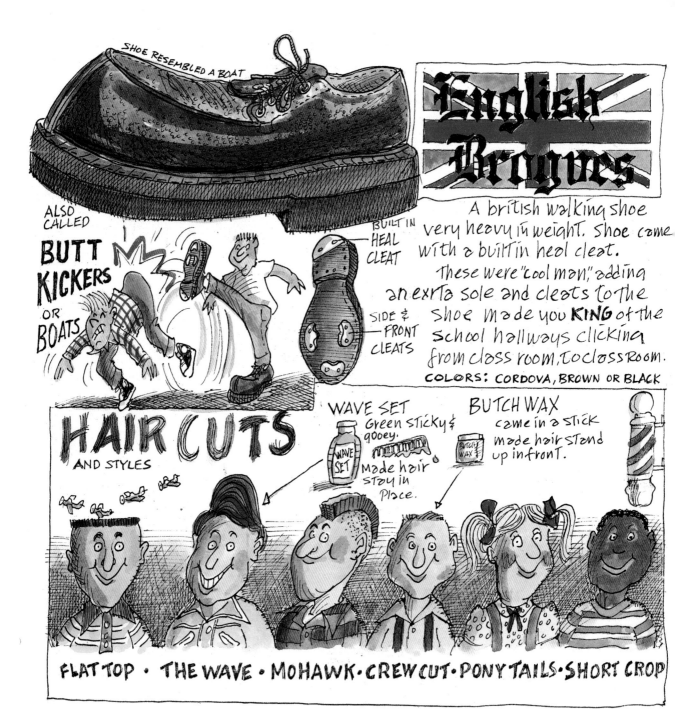

SHOE RESEMBLED A BOAT

English Brogues

ALSO CALLED

BUTT KICKERS

OR **BOATS**

BUILT IN HEAL CLEAT

SIDE & FRONT CLEATS

A british walking shoe very heavy in weight. Shoe came with a built in heel cleat.

These were "cool man," adding an exrta sole and cleats to the shoe made you **KING** of the school hallways clicking from class room, to class room.

COLORS: CORDOVA, BROWN OR BLACK

HAIR CUTS
AND STYLES

WAVE SET Green sticky & gooey. Made hair stay in place.

BUTCH WAX came in a stick made hair stand up in front.

FLAT TOP · THE WAVE · MOHAWK · CREW CUT · PONY TAILS · SHORT CROP

GETTING HIGH

Getting high was bouncing on a pogo stick, walking on home-made stilts, climbing trees, walking on coffee tins.

COFFEE TINS TIED AROUND SHOES WITH THICK STRING OR TWINE

HOLE

THE POWERFULL **WHAM-O** SLING SHOT

DEAD EYE FOR ACCURACY

BEECH-NUT-GUM

A LONG TASTING CHEWING GUM 1950'S

May Basket

ON MAY DAY YOU PLACED A BASKET OF FLOWERS NEXT TO THE FRONT DOOR, RANG THE DOOR BELL AND RAN OFF TO HIDE.
THE BASKET WAS GIVEN TO SOMEONE VERY SPECIAL.

WAX MUSTACHE, LIPS

and TEETH

Black

white

Red

BELT LOOP DECOR

rabbits foot (good luck)

Plastic Puzzles

The wax would taste sweet while chewing Then you spit it out.

BEADS & GIMP

WIRE

BEADS

You could make a ring, Bracelet or necklace

NIK-L-LIPS

Miniature Wax bottles filled with syrup.

TAR CHEWING

Burner was used to melt tar.

Tar came in bricks with paper casing

Tar was also used to patch cracks on city streets. On hot summer days the tar got soft and you could pinch a piece off and chew.

IT WAS FUN TO FOLLOW THE CRACKS ON YOUR BIKE LIKE A ROAD MAP.

HAPPY CHEWING

YUMMM!

Chewing tar was a treat.
Roofers would use the tar for laying shingles and patch work on roofs. If you asked for a piece of tar the roofer would gladly cut a piece off and hand it to you. The tar had a very bland and flat taste.
~ I don't think this would pass FDA regulations today. ~

CLOTHESPIN MATCH GUN

RUBBER BAND HOLDS THE TWO HALVES OF CLOTHES-PIN TOGETHER

PULL SPRING (TRIGGER) BACK TO SHOOT MATCH

WHEN SPRING IS PULLED BACK THIS PART THRUSTS FORWARD, LIGHTING AND PROJECTING MATCH

SPRING IS IN COCKED POSITION

REGULAR CLOTHES PIN

If grass was dry and uncut a small brush fire could start. BOY! That got you in trouble.

USE STRIKE ANYWHERE WOODEN MATCHES

Cereal Box Tops

EXLPORER'S RING

COMPASS AND SUN DIAL

ONLY 25¢ AND THE BOX TOP FROM THIS PACKAGE

FITS ANY FINGER

GRAPE=NUTS FLAKES Post Cereals

DIVING SUBMARINE

SUBMARINE WAS CHARGED WITH BAKING POWDER

SUBMARINE WAS 3" LONG CAME IN GRAY AND MADE ABOUT 12 DIVES WITH A SINGLE CHARGE OF BAKING POWDER

NABISCO SHREDDED WHEAT
NABISCO SHREDDED WHEAT

SKY KING RADAR SIGNAL RING
THIS RING WAS 15¢ AND ONE ROUND METAL DISC FROM A PETER PAN PEANUT BUTTER JAR.

By sending in money along with a box top cereal companys offered many types of gadgets for kids.

THESE CARDBOARD STRIPS THAT SEPARATED EACH ROW OF SHREDDED WHEAT INSIDE BOX HAD GAMES, CUTOUTS AND COMIC STRIPS PRINTED ON THEM.

IT WAS SO EXCITING TO RECEIVE YOUR ORDER.

DELIVERY TIME ABOUT 3 WEEKS

A) PLACE SUBMARINE IN WATER
B) SUBMARINE DIVES TO BOTTOM.
C) BAKING POWDER BUBBLES, SUBMARINE RISES TO SURFACE.
D) SUBMARINE REPEATS PROCESS.

END VIEW OF BATH TUB

14

WE PLAYED

COWBOYS AND INDIANS

BANG!

War paint was used with Lipstick and burnt cork.

The sound of caps meant school was out. AND SO WAS THE DOG

Tape handle

Tree branch Bow

WOODEN BULLETS

BACK OF HOLSTER

Six Gun
CAP PISTOL

LOAD CAPS HERE

TEXAS

HAMMER

Barrel release

Caps emitted a sulfer odor when popped

ARROW MADE WITH BRANCH (HOMEMADE)

ARROW WITH METAL TIP

ARROW WITH RUBBER TIP

CAPS 5 ROLLS

BOX OF CAPS

Entire roll made big bang

Gun handle or a rock was used for hitting caps on sidewalk.

We played on the sidewalk and street

THE OLD STREET ARC LIGHT WAS REPLACED BY THE ARGON LIGHT IN 1955

HERE I COME READY OR NOT!

HIDE & GO SEEK

HOME PLATE

FIRST BASE

HOP SCOTCH

BALL AND JACKS

MAN HOLE COVER BECAME PITCHER'S MOUND

THIRD BASE

SECOND BASE

FLAG FOOTBALL AND TOUCH FOOTBALL

A METAL STRAP FROM A NAIL KEG WAS USED FOR A BASKETBALL HOOP

NAILED TO TELEPHONE POLE

NAILS

POCKET MAGNIFYING GLASS

BY USING THE SUN RAYS YOU COULD START A FIRE

BURNING BUGS AND YOUR FRIEND WAS NOT A GOOD THING!

TAPING A BALL

LACES

STITCHES

COVER

BLACK ELECTRICAL FRICTION TAPE

AT TIMES THE STITCHING WORE OUT CAUSING THE BALL TO FALL APART. FRICTION TAPE SOLVED THE PROBLEM.

SQUIRREL KNOB OR SUICIDE KNOB

KNUCKLE BUSTER

LOOKED COOL BUT SERVED NO PURPOSE FOR STEERING

MOUNTED ON THE WHEEL THE KNOB MADE TURNING EASIER. THEY WERE CONSIDERED DANGEROUS DUE TO COAT AND SHIRT SLEEVE GETTING CAUGHT.

PRINCE ALBERT WAS AMERICA'S LARGEST SELLING SMOKING TOBACCO.

DO YOU HAVE PRINCE ALBERT IN A CAN?

YES

WELL YOU BETTER LET HIM OUT!

PHONE GAGS

On a boring day calling random phone numbers and telling silly jokes passed the time away.

AFTER TELLING JOKE YOU HUNG UP IMMEDIATELY.

ANOTHER GAG LINE WAS: IS YOUR REFRIGERATOR RUNNING?...(YES) WELL YOU BETTER GO CATCH IT BEFORE IT RUNS AWAY!

I LIKE IKE

DWIGHT EISENHOWER (REPUBLICAN) AND ADLAI STEVENSON (DEMOCRAT) CAMPAIGNED FOR PRESIDENT IN 1952

EISENHOWER CAMPAIGN BUTTON

IN 1952 THE THREE MAJOR NETWORKS TELEVISED THE CONVENTION. VERY FEW AMERICANS OWNED T.V. SETS. TO ACCOMMODATE THE PUBLIC, SOME DEPT. STORES PLACED T.V. SETS IN THEIR WINDOWS WHICH ALSO PROMOTED TELEVISION SALES.

VOTING BOOTH

VOTING PRECINCT

DURING AN ELECTION YEAR A HOME OWNER COULD RENT OUT THE FAMILY BASEMENT AS A VOTING PRECINCT. THE CITY PAYED THE OWNER.

Keds AND P.F. FLIERS TENNIS SHOES

THESE TENNIS SHOES COULD NOT BE WORN IN SCHOOL ONLY IN GYM CLASS.

VOTE HERE

STEEL RIMS
WOODEN SPOKES

PAPER ROUTE

HAND ROLLED NEWSPAPER THROWN ON FRONT PORCH

OREGON

EARLY IN THE MORNING NEWSPAPERS WERE DELIVERED ON BICYCLES AND WAGONS BY THE PAPER BOY

TIMES HERALD

THE CHRISTMAS TREE

TREE WAS ALWAYS TOO TALL

Dad smoked

Every year dad would drill holes in the main stem of the tree. He put branches in the holes to fill in the bare spots. Mom supervised the event.

Before there were cultured tree farms trees were cut in the wild with imperfections, such as, bare spots and crooked main stems.

AT THE TREE LOT YOU COULD GET FREE BRANCHES TO FILL IN THE SCARCE AREAS

NOMA BUBBLE-LITES

THE LIGHTS WERE FIRST MARKETED IN 1945 BY THE NOMA ELECTRIC CO. THE HEAT FROM THE BULB BOILS THE LIQUID TO CREATE THE BUBBLING ACTION.

ALUMINUM TREE

TREE WOULD ROTATE

COLOR WHEEL TURNED AND PROJECTED DIFFERENT COLORS ON TREE.

PLASTIC ICICLES

PLASTIC REPLACED THE FOIL ICICLE DURING WWII BECAUSE OF METAL SHORTAGES. WE STILL USED PLASTIC INTO THE LATE 40'S

*ALSO CALLED RAIN

THE Christmas window

Every year at Christmas one of the major dept. stores would present an animated christmas display in the window.

DUCK AND COVER

THE FEAR OF AN ATOMIC BOMB ATTACK WAS REALLY SCARY IN THE EARLY 50's. HERE ARE SIX SURVIVAL SECRETS FOR ATOMIC BOMB ATTACKS."

1. TAKE COVER.
2. DROP FLAT.
3. BURY FACE IN ARMS.
4. DON'T RUSH OUTSIDE AFTER THE BOMBING... WAIT.
5. BEWARE, FOOD, WATER.
6. DON'T START RUMORS.

Bomb drills were common in the classroom. "DUCK AND COVER"!

ATOMIC DEFENSE Sirens

Sirens were located on top of tall bldgs.

3 short sirens - take cover

1 long siren - all-clear

WE'RE GOING TO BE KILLED!

Siren would blast about 3 min.

On some days at 12:00 noon the siren would BLAST! Some people would panic and forget that it was just a test.

THE CIVIL DEFENSE TEAM

CIVILIAN DEFENSE VOLUNTEERS

Some department stores would have a record dept. The listening room was where records could be listened to before being purchased. The rooms were sound proof and time limits were strictly enforced.

In 1948 the 45-RPM and 33-RPM records caused the 78-RPM to go obsolete.

You would never turn your friends down for a bike ride.

LIK-M-AID tasted like flavored sugar with a Tart taste. You would pour the sugar in your hand and lick leaving a stain on the hand and Tongue.

• WE USED TO SPELL IT "LICK-A-MAID"

Shoe store Fluoroscopes

1940's 1950's

The Fluoroscope was an X-Ray that was used to show how your foot fit within the shoe. The shoe store fluoroscopes were outlawed in most states in the late 50's due to health risks.

VIEW PORTS

Both customer and salesperson, had to lean over cabinet of the fluoroscope to look in through viewports. The machine would cast a light green tint.

We used to "wiggle" our toes. for the fun of it.

This is what you would see.

Comic Book AND Lemonade STANDS

1953 NASH AMBASSADOR CUSTOM COUNTRY CLUB 2-DOOR HARDTOP

DING DING

ROBIN HOOD

SUPERMAN

RAGGEDY ANN AND ANDY

TOM SAWYER

COMICS 5¢ TODAY 2¢

LEMON ADE 10¢

This is how we made extra pocket money by selling comics and lemonade

RED LEFT BLUE RIGHT
DIMENSIONAL VIEWER

THEY REACH OUT AND TOUCH YOU

3-D HOLLYWOOD PIN UPS

3-D COMIC BOOKS

THIS IS WHAT YOU WOULD SEE BEFORE WEARING VIEWER.

DURING THE 3-D MOVIE BOOM SOME COMICS WERE PRINTED IN 3-D

PHOTOS WERE ALSO PRINTED IN 3-D SUCH AS HOLLYWOOD PIN-UPS 1953

ANOTHER ICE CREAM SERVICE WAS CALLED THE GOOD HUMOUR MAN.

YOU COULD GET A PIECE OF DRY ICE FREE

MONEY POUCH

When hearing the bell kids ran home to get a dime from their mom.

THE JO-JO WAGON

In the summer the Jo-Jo wagon rode by selling ice cream bars.

DING DING

JO-JO BARS 10¢

CRUNCHY 10¢

LINED METAL BOX FILLED WITH DRY ICE AND ICE CREAM BARS

IN THE EARLY 50's COMICS SOLD FOR 10¢ TO 15¢ EA. 3-D's SOLD FOR 35¢ EA.

27

HOME MILK DELIVERY

UMMM... LICK LICK

HEAVY PAPER TOP

CRIMPED SIDES

PULL TAB — LID MADE OF CARD BOARD

THE LICK

THE LID FIT 3/16" BELOW LIP OF BOTTLE

GLASS BOTTLE

The cream raised to the top, settling on the bottom of lid. before drinking you would lick the thick rich cream off. **YUM!**

MILK WAS DELIVERED TO YOUR DOOR STEP EARLY IN THE MORNING.

SUNRISE DAIRY

CLINK CLINK CLINK

The Milkman wore a white shirt, pants and a black bow Tie. He stood when driving the Truck.

Milk was put into a metal or masonite box next to your door

Empty Bottles were re-cycled and used again.

Eggs, cream, butter and butter milk were also available.

THE CLINKING NOISE FROM THE BOTTLES COULD BE HEARD UP AND DOWN THE BLOCK.

Soda Fountain Drinks

PAPER STRAWS →

MILK SHAKES AND CHOCOLATE MALTS

IT WAS RUMORED THAT COKE COMBINED WITH ASPIRIN WOULD GET YOU HIGH.

NOT TRUE

VANILLA, CHOCOLATE AND CHERRY COKES

CHERRY & LIME PHOSPHATES

GREEN RIVER

CHOCOLATE AND ROOT BEER FLOATS.

BASIC FLAVORS STRAWBERRY·VANILLA·CHOCOLATE

28

BACKYARD CLOTHES LINE

Clothes lines were used for blanket tents. We would sit inside reading comic books and sipping Kool aid.

HELLO

PIPE WAS HOLLOW YELLING THROUGH THE HOLE WAS A KICK

TWO BLANKETS ATTACHED AT TOP

HANGING ON THE CLOTHES LINE WAS A NO! NO!

ESCAPE ROUTE TO NEIGHBORS BACK YARD

SOMETIMES CLIMBING OVER A FENCE YOUR FOOT WOULD GET STUCK.

WHEELS, BRICKS ETC. WERE USED FOR WEIGHTS

MOM!

KITCHEN CUBBYHOLE VENTS

CIRCULATING AIR FROM OUTSIDE

THE ICE MAN COMETH

Some homes still required a block of ice for refrigeration. When ice was needed a number was placed in the window.

ON HOT SUMMER DAYS IT WAS WONDERFUL TO SUCK ON A PIECE OF ICE. CLEAN, COOL AND REFRESHING. GIMMIE GIMMIE GIMMIE

LEATHER SHOULDER PROTECTOR

INSIDE THE CUBBY-HOLE TWO SMALL SCREENED WINDOW VENTS KEPT FOOD COOL.

VENTS

CURB FEELER'S

Curb feeler's were used to judge the distance between the automobile and curb when parking. They made a high pitched scraping noise so you could tell how close to the curb you were.

Curb feeler's were purchased by an older group of people.

A good way to keep white walls clean.

1951 Hudson Hornet

FLIPPING BOTTLE CAPS

SNAP

WOW!

With snap of finger cap would take off.

Soda Pop Machine

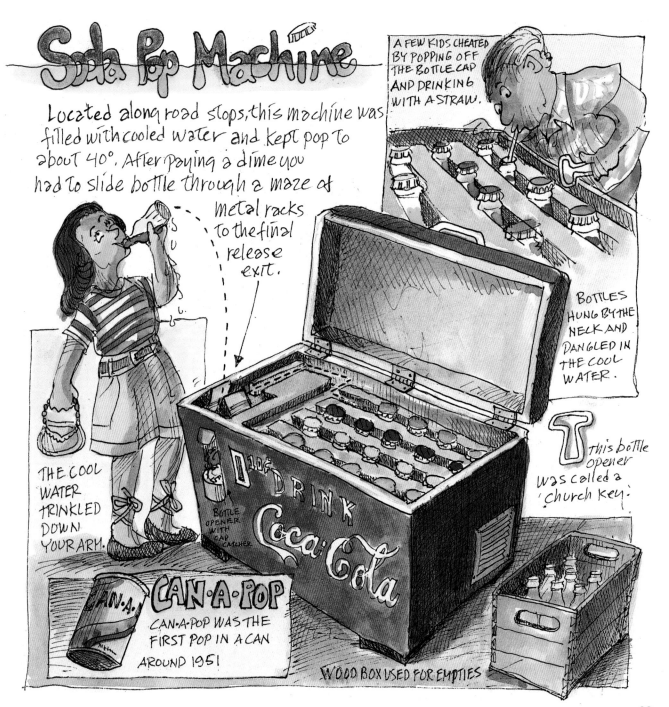

Located along road stops, this machine was filled with cooled water and kept pop to about 40°. After paying a dime you had to slide bottle through a maze of metal racks to the final release exit.

A FEW KIDS CHEATED BY POPPING OFF THE BOTTLE CAP AND DRINKING WITH A STRAW.

BOTTLES HUNG BY THE NECK AND DANGLED IN THE COOL WATER.

THE COOL WATER TRINKLED DOWN YOUR ARM.

This bottle opener was called a 'church key'.

10¢ DRINK Coca-Cola

BOTTLE OPENER WITH CAP CATCHER

CAN·A·POP WAS THE FIRST POP IN A CAN AROUND 1951

WOOD BOX USED FOR EMPTIES

ANNIE ANNIE OVER!

After saying "Annie Annie over" ball was thrown over house to your friend on the receiving end.

CUSTOM BIKE

To be different some kids customized their bicycles.

CUT OFF ENDS OF HANDLE GRIPS AND SLIDE UP HANDLE

REVERSED HANDLE BARS

DUAL REFLECTORS

RAISED SEAT

FENDERS REMOVED

REMOVE CHAIN GUARD

REMOVE KICK STAND

PEDAL OFTEN FELL APART AND JUST HUNG THERE

GAMES WE ~PLAYED~

LIGHT LIGHT

- MOTHER MAY I?
- RED ROVER, RED ROVER
- SIMON SAYS
- KICK THE CAN
- HIDE AND SEEK
- DODGEBALL · KICKBALL
- HOPSCOTCH
- LEAP FROG
- JACKS

JOHNNY! IT'S TIME TO COME IN.

When it was time to come in from playing Mom called out your first name. If you ignored her she called out your first and last name. If you still did not respond she called out your FIRST MIDDLE and LAST NAME loud and firm! If that still did not work, DAD solved the problem.

WITHOUT A CHAIN GUARD THE PANT LEG GOT CAUGHT IN THE CHAIN AND RIPPED YOUR PANTS

ROLLING THE PANT LEG UP DID SOLVE THE PROBLEM.

A METAL CLIP WAS ALSO USED FOR PANT LEG.

HAND CARVED YO YO's

OCCASIONALLY A MAN FROM THE ISLANDS APPEARED AT THE LOCAL FIVE & DIME STORE TO CARVE A DESIGN ON YOUR NEW PURCHASED YO YO.

34

TEXACO
1948 LOGO

FULL SERVICE AND THEN SOME

Gas stations went all out for the customer along with good service free glassware, prizes, balloons etc. were handed out to lure the customer back.

1951 CRANBROOK BELVEDERE 2 DOOR HARDTOP - PLYMOUTH

TEXACO OPENED ITS FIRST "FILLING STATION" IN 1911

FLYING A
Mobilgas
SHELL
OTHER GAS DEALERSHIPS

THE TEXACO STAR THEATER STARRING MILTON BERLE AIRED ON TELEVISION IN 1948

IT WAS SAID ABOUT THE STUDEBAKER YOU CAN'T TELL IF IT'S COMIN OR GOIN.

NO IRONING NECESSARY

METAL ADJUSTABLE FRAMES

AFTER WASHING PANTS INSERT FRAMES

PANTS HAD TO BE DAMP

WHEN PANTS DRY REMOVE FRAMES

WHAT A CREASE!

WRINGER WAS USED TO PRESS WATER OUT OF CLOTHES.

THE 1947 NORGE "RO-TA-TOR" WASHER"

RUBBER PENCIL TRICK

HOLD PENCIL LOOSELY WITH INDEX FINGER AND THUMB

SHAKE UP AND DOWN GENTLY CREATING AN ILLUSION OF A RUBBER PENCIL.

CLOTHES SPRINKLER

CORK

SHIRTS WERE SPRINKLED WHILE IRONING.

POP BOTTLE FILLED WITH WATER

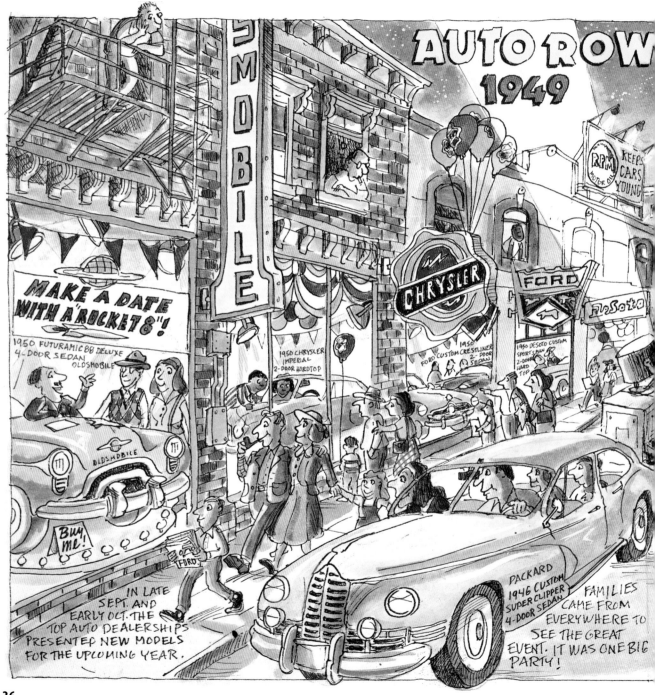

PEDAL BLOCKS

When a bike was handed down to a younger sister or brother wood blocks were placed on pedals so feet could reach pedal

WOOD BLOCKS

BOLT

Drilled HOLE

* ALSO USED ON TRICYCLES

WASHER

NUT

PEDAL

SHEEPS WOOL SEAT COVER

Problem was rain got seat soaked and so was your bottom.

Saddle Shoes

SADDLE CLEANER AND POLISH

WHITE

WHITE LIQUID TO COVER SCUFF MARKS

Butter cup

Place Dandelion under chin if reflection turns yellow (which always occurred) you were very much in LOVE!

CHUBBIES

JEANS MADE FOR PLUMP BOYS

HEARING AID WITH POCKET BATTERY EARLY 1950s

REINFORCED DOUBLE KNEE PADS

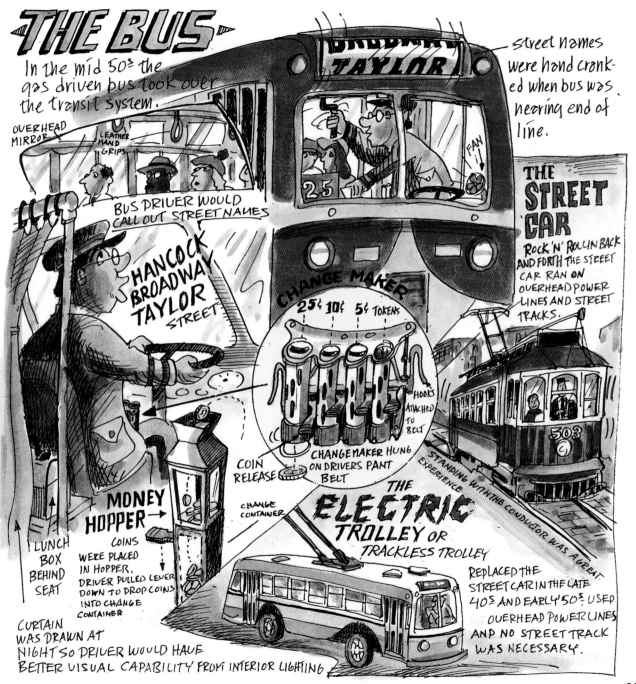

THE BUS

In the mid 50s the gas driven bus took over the transit system.

street names were hand cranked when bus was nearing end of line.

OVERHEAD MIRROR

LEATHER HAND GRIPS

BROADWAY TAYLOR

25

FAN

BUS DRIVER WOULD CALL OUT STREET NAMES

HANCOCK BROADWAY TAYLOR street

THE STREET CAR

ROCK 'N' ROLLIN BACK AND FORTH THE STREET CAR RAN ON OVERHEAD POWER LINES AND STREET TRACKS.

CHANGE MAKER

25¢ 10¢ 5¢ TOKENS

HOOKS ATTACHED TO BELT

503

CHANGEMAKER HUNG ON DRIVERS PANT BELT

COIN RELEASE

CHANGE CONTAINER

STANDING WITH THE CONDUCTOR WAS A GREAT EXPERIENCE

THE ELECTRIC TROLLEY OR TRACKLESS TROLLEY

MONEY HOPPER →

COINS WERE PLACED IN HOPPER, DRIVER PULLED LEVER DOWN TO DROP COINS INTO CHANGE CONTAINER

LUNCH BOX BEHIND SEAT

REPLACED THE STREET CAR IN THE LATE 40s AND EARLY '50s USED OVERHEAD POWER LINES AND NO STREET TRACK WAS NECESSARY.

CURTAIN WAS DRAWN AT NIGHT SO DRIVER WOULD HAVE BETTER VISUAL CAPABILITY FROM INTERIOR LIGHTING

40

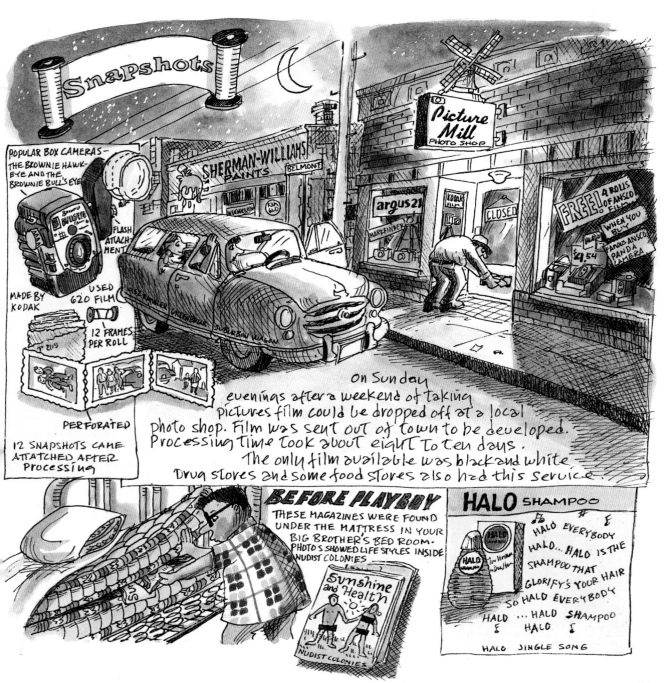

Snapshots

POPULAR BOX CAMERAS—
THE BROWNIE HAWK-
EYE AND THE
BROWNIE BULL'S EYE

FLASH ATTACHMENT

MADE BY KODAK

USED 620 FILM

12 FRAMES PER ROLL

PERFORATED

12 SNAPSHOTS CAME ATTACHED AFTER PROCESSING

SHERMAN-WILLIAMS PAINTS

BELMONT

WEATHERTEX

Picture Mill PHOTO SHOP

argus 21

HARFINDER

KODAK FILM

CLOSED

FREE! 4 ROLLS OF ANSCO FILM WHEN YOU BUY FAMOUS ANSCO PANDA CAMERA

$4.54

On Sunday evenings after a weekend of taking pictures film could be dropped off at a local photo shop. Film was sent out of town to be developed. Processing time took about eight to ten days. The only film available was black and white. Drug stores and some food stores also had this service.

BEFORE PLAYBOY
THESE MAGAZINES WERE FOUND UNDER THE MATTRESS IN YOUR BIG BROTHER'S BED ROOM. PHOTOS SHOWED LIFE STYLES INSIDE NUDIST COLONIES

Sunshine and Health
NUDIST COLONIES

HALO SHAMPOO

HALO EVERYBODY HALO... HALO IS THE SHAMPOO THAT GLORIFY'S YOUR HAIR SO HALO EVERYBODY HALO... HALO SHAMPOO HALO

HALO JINGLE SONG

41

WOTCHING THE RADIO

1941 PHILCO UPRIGHT RADIO

MOM DOING THE HULA

DAD PLUNKING ON THE UKULELE

If you like-a Uk-u-le-le La-dy, Uk-u-le-le La-dy like - a you -

HAWAII CALLS

ZENITH TABLE RADIO

Every Saturday evening the radio show named Hawaii Calls broadcast from The Moana Hotel Banyan Lanai in Waikiki. The show originated in 1935. The music faded in and out like ocean waves.

THE AMOS 'N' ANDY SHOW

NBC

SPEAKING IN BLACK VOICE AMOS 'N' ANDY WERE TWO WHITE COMICS

THE EDGAR BERGEN AND CHARLIE McCARTHY SHOW

NBC

THE VENTRILOQUIST EDGAR CRACKED JOKES WITH HIS DUMMY CHARLIE

SOME OF THE PROGRAMS

- SGT. PRESTON OF THE YUKON
- SKY KING
- THE WHISTLER
- NO SCHOOL TODAY
- BURNS AND ALLEN
- THE LONE RANGER
- FIBBER McGEE AND MOLLY
- LUX RADIO THEATRE
- DUFFY'S TAVERN

RADIO VACUUM TUBE

- THE BICKERSONS
- JACK BENNY
- THE SHADOW
- INNER SANCTUM
- DON McNEIL AND THE BREAKFAST CLUB
- FRED ALLEN

Driving along the highway families encountered these six small humorous panel signs stuck in the ground promoting the product **BURMA-SHAVE**. **BURMA-SHAVE** signs started appearing along road sides since 1926.

Burma-Shave
BY USING
THAN BEFORE
SIX MORE MINUTES
NOW CAN SNORE
EVERY SHAVER

Signs were 100 paces apart.

BEFORE BUMPER STICKERS
Tourist sites put on cardboard signs for advertising.

CARDBOARD SIGN TIED ON BUMPER WITH WIRE. USUALLY PUT ON FRONT BUMPER

UNCANNY CANYON

TREES OF MYSTERY
Sea lion caves
STUDEBAKER 1949

43

CANVAS WATER BAG

60 DAYS

1948 Fleetline Chevrolet

A canvas water bag was hung on the front bumper in the event of an overheating radiator on long trips.

CANDY CIGARETTES FILLED WITH CHOCOLATE

WATER

Chocolate CIGARETTES

POLE SITTING

Some individuals would sit on top of a pole for days so they could be the record holders

STREET CLEANERS

LEAVES WERE SWEPT IN SMALL PILES ALONG THE CURB FOLLOWED BY A TRUCK WITH A CITY WORKER STANDING ON A PLATFORM SCOOPING LEAVES INTO THE TRUCK.

STACK OF WOOD ALONG CURBSIDE FOR WOOD FURNACE

LADY IN PEN

LADY STANDS FULLY DRESSED IN PEN. TURN PEN UPSIDE DOWN FOR A FEW SECONDS. TURN PEN BACK TO UPRIGHT POSITION LADYS CLOTHES MYSTERIOUSLY DISAPPEAR

LIQUID INSIDE

PEN WAS USUALLY FOUND IN DAD'S DESK DRAWER

HEAT

THE MAIN SOURCE OF FUEL WAS WOOD AND COAL IN AMERICAN HOMES

SAW-DUST BURNER

SAWDUST

HOPPER

PENDULUM USED TO REGULATE THE FLOW OF SAWDUST

BURNER

WATER

SAWDUST BIN

WADDED UP NEWSPAPER STUFFED IN BURNER THEN LIT.

COAL CHUTES WERE USED THROUGH BASEMENT WINDOWS ALSO.

COAL

THE COAL MAN TRANSFERRED SACKS OF COAL FROM THE TRUCK TO THE BASEMENT COAL BIN.

BURNING COAL CREATED A THICK BLUISH-BLACK SMOKE. IT STUNK!

HOPPER HAD TO BE FILLED ABOUT 3-4 TIMES DAILY

MADE YOU GAG FOR AIR

EARLY CELL PHONE

HELLO

HELLO

ATTACH STRING TO THE BOTTOM OF 2 EMPTY CANS, STRETCH TIGHT, THEN TALK.

PAPER CUPS WORKED TOO

CUT AWAY SHOWING INSIDE OF THE TUBE

WHIZZ

PNEUMATIC TUBES

OR MONEY CHUTE$

The pneumatic Tube was used in dept. stores to transfer money up to the accounting office on the top floor. change was made and sent back down the tube to the sales clerk

SALE

HATS

CONTAINERS MADE A WHIZZING SOUND WHILE TRAVELING THROUGH THE VACUUM TUBES.

METAL CONTAINER WOULD LAND IN A BASKET WITH A WHOOSH AND PLONK.

METAL CONTAINER WHERE MONEY WAS PLACED

RUBBER ENDS

REVOLVING CHARGE CARD

Sears AND Roebuck 042610.7 JOHN DOE

A METAL CHARGE CARD TO BE USED ONLY AT THE DEPT. STORE YOU WERE SHOPPING. CAME WITH LEATHER CASE.

THE STARTER

Clicking her clicker the starter would direct you to the nearest available elevator.

THIS CARS GOING UP!

CLICK CLICK

ELEVATOR OPERATOR

TIN CLICKER OR WOODEN CASTANETS WERE USED

IT WOULD TAKE 2-3 TIMES FOR OPERATOR TO LEVEL ELEVATOR

ESCALATORS CAME ABOUT 1954-55

ELEVATOR OPERATOR WOULD CALL OUT THE FLOORS MEN'S WOMENS CLOTHES, TOY DEPT. ETC.

46

THE CORNER MARKET

HANDY MARKET

FRESH APPLES 10¢

TOMATO 25¢ SACK

AN EXTENSION DEVICE AND LADDER ON WHEELS WERE USED FOR HARD TO GET ITEMS.

ON THE CUFF
GROCERY BILL WAS PAID ONCE A WEEK ON PAY DAY

DARK WOOD FLOORS

BUTCHER SHOP

A spool of string hung from the ceiling for wrapping butcher paper around meat.
BUTCHER PAPER

PAPER TAPE

WET SPONGE FOR TAPE

CLEAN EMPTY MEAT TRAYS

WIND, RAIN, SNOW, OR HEAT DIDN'T STOP THE ...

DELIVERY BOY

DELIVERY - ONE MILE RADIUS

HANDY MARKET

OVER SIZE WIRE BASKET

METAL CLIP TO KEEP PANT LEG UP. TO AVOID GREASE STAINS FROM CHAIN

After school and all day Saturday the delivery boy brought groceries to your house.

STORES WERE CLOSED ON SUNDAYS

CLOSED ON SUNDAY

SAWDUST FLOOR COVERING

KICK STAND

Behind the meat counter sawdust covered the floors to absorb the meat drippings. Every Saturday night the old sawdust was removed and new fresh sawdust was raked in.

EARS WERE THE RESTING PLACE FOR THE PENCIL

THE MOVIES 25¢

It was common to enter the theater in the middle of a movie and exit where you came in. We had a double feature, cartoon, and a news reel (eyes and ears of the world)

LOGES

Located in the back of the theater Cost - 20¢

Seats could Rock

Extreme comfort But not affordable for a majority of movie goers.

THE LONE RANGER RIDES AGAIN

SATURDAY MATINEE

FLASH LIGHT WITH RED SHADE

SHINY SILK UNIFORM

THE BALCONY

Some kids dropped Popcorn, threw Gum wrapper planes and Popped their bubble GUM.

USHERETTES

Would escort you to your Seat.

GUM

CUP STOMPING BANG! and out of the theater you went.

CAUTION

KABOOM!

HANDLE BAR CANNON

Remove handle grips insert cork ball followed by a fire cracker and potato. Jam potato in hard and fast to block entry way. As fire cracker goes off the cork ball projects out the other end of handle.

HANDLE BAR GRIPS

STREAMERS

Plastic streamers were attached to handle grips

POPULAR BICYCLES

1948 MONARCH SUPER DELUXE

OFFERED ONE FULL YEAR OF FIRE AND THEFT INSURANCE WITH EVERY BICYCLE

1949 DONALD DUCK BICYCLE

DONALD'S EYES WOULD BLINK OR STAY ON AS A HEADLIGHT. THE ELECTRIC HORN WENT "QUACK-QUACK!"

1950's SCHWINN BLACK PHANTOM SPRING FORK

THE MOST POPULAR BICYCLE EVER IN AMERICA. THIS WAS TO DIE FOR! IT HAD CHROME ON RIMS, TANK, FENDERS AND MOST OF ALL A KNEE-ACTION SPRING FORK.

SHIRT PINS

Remove pressed cork from back of bottle cap. Place cap on front of shirt and the cork on back then press.

Most Bottle caps had a cork backing

— Mohawk haircut

Police knife
(To remove cork)

LUCKY STRIKE!

If you found the brand name LUCKY STRIKE cigarettes lying on the ground you would step on it, sock your friend saying "**LUCKY STRIKE!**" no strike back!

WINDOW AIR Swamp Cooler

1951 CRANBROOK BELVEDERE 2-DOOR HARDTOP PLYMOUTH

PLYMOUTH

CARSON CITY NEVADA

CALIFORNIA 51 82B 6135

These were popular before air conditioning was available on cars. They were mounted on the passenger side high in the window. On real hot days you could add crushed ice to really cool things down. Cooler would drop temperature in the car 20° cooler than outside. They were sold by Montgomery Wards and Allstate (Sears).

INTAKE VENT

CAP

WINDOW CLIPS

COOL AIR VENTS

METAL SUN VISOR

PRISM

DASHBOARD PRISM

SOME CARS HAD METAL SUN VISORS OVER THE WIND SHIELD WHICH MADE VIEWING THE TRAFFIC LIGHT VERY DIFFICULT. A PRISM WAS PUT ON THE DASH SO TRAFFIC LIGHT COULD BE SEEN.

With red measles you were told to close the window shades, keep the room dark to protect your eyes.

THE DOCTOR MADE HOUSE CALLS

When you were sick the Doctor would come to your house and treat the illness. Night visits were common.

Through toughest conditions the doctor would always be there.

REMEDY FOR EAR ACHE

Tie knot in sock

Fill sock with salt, place in oven heat, then place sock on ear.

PEPTO-BISMOL
Still used today.
FOR NAUSEA

GERITOL
MOM TOOK THIS.
FOR VITALITY.

COD LIVER OIL
FOR VITAMIN INTAKE (YUK!)

• HOUSE HOLD ITEMS •

STRETCH OR MUMBLETYPEG

GIMP NECKLACE

The object of this game was to stand face to face taking turns flipping a pocket knife into the ground. First one who could not reach the knife with their foot lost the game.

EACH TOSS WAS ABOUT 12" APART.

OLEO MARGARINE

CAPSULE

WHITE MARGARINE

Oleo Margarine was a butter substitute and was white in color. To look like real butter a capsule of orange-yellow powder was added and mixed in the bowl to create a golden yellow color

Canned Feet

CLOMP CLOMP

By crushing 2 empty cans with your feet the cans stuck to the soles of your shoes making lots of noise stomping down the sidewalk.

YOUR BUDDY PUSHED FROM BEHIND

ORANGE CRATE

HOT ROD!

Trying to find the right axle length for the wheels was a challenge.

EVERY SUMMER THE SOAP BOX DERBY

OLD TRICYCLE WHEELS

ROPE STEERING

FOOT BRACE

HAND BRAKE (NEVER WORKED)

OLD WAGON WHEELS

TIN CAN HEAD-LIGHTS

NUT, BOLT & WASHER IN FRONT WAS USED SO CRATE COULD TURN.

Crude and awkward was practically impossible to steer.

BASIC HOME MADE SCOOTER

THE SCOOTER

MADE OUT OF METAL PAINTED GRAY. WHAT MORE CAN I SAY?

LIGHT

HANDLE

APPLE CRATE BOX

KICK-STAND

REFLECTOR

ROLLER SKATES ATTACHED TO A 2' BY 4'

RUBBER PAD

WHITE WALL WHEELS

On Sunday evenings we would drive to the airport and watch the planes take off and land.

POOL TUBES

INNER TUBES WERE BLACK SOME WERE LIGHT RED.

ROLLING HUGE TRUCK INNER TUBES TO THE CITY PARK SWIMMING POOL.

INNER TUBES WERE ON YARDS ALL SUMMER LONG.

ROLLING DOWN HILL IN AN INNER TUBE

PATCH FOR LEAK

THE TREASURED ITEM FOR BOY'S

DAISY No 25b B.B. GUN 1952

—NO 300 TELESCOPE SIGHT

OTHER STYLE WAS THE RED RYDER B.B. GUN

Catching Bees in Hollyhocks

CATCH A BEE IN A HOLLYHOCK FLOWER!

BREAK OFF STEM HOLD FLOWER TO EAR AND LISTEN.

CLOSE FLOWER SLOWLY TRAPPING BEE INSIDE

WHEN THE BEE STOPS BUZZING SIMPLY SHAKE THE FLOWER AND THE BEE WILL START BUZZING AGAIN.

BZZZZZZ

CATCHING BUGS IN JARS

FIELD GRASSHOPPER-SPITTING

GARDEN GROUND BEETLE

WE CALLED IT GRASSHOPPER SPIT OR TOBACCO JUICE YUK!

SIDE VIEW MIRROR

SILVER SPOT LIGHT

HORN

RING RING

SILVER BELL

WIRE BASKET ON FRONT

FENDER LIGHT

SPEED ODOMETER

BIKE RACK

CHAIN GUARD

MUD FLAPS WITH reflectors

MOTOR BIKE

Simply attach cards on the fender supports with a clothes pin.

When wheels turned the cards flipped off the spokes creating a motor sound.

KICK STAND

With heavy use the cards eventually weakened the spokes.

THE 4 PARTY LINE

The party line is when you shared your telephone line with other customers. Private lines were available but very expensive. The more parties the less you paid. Party lines had their draw backs, there always was someone on the telephone line.

The average household had 2 party lines.

IT WAS QUITE COMMON TO LISTEN IN ON THE OTHER PARTY'S GOSSIP.

ALL PHONES WERE BLACK

THE PACIFIC TELEPHONE & TELEGRAPH CO.
AMERICAN TELEPHONE & TELEGRAPH CO.
BELL SYSTEM

AMERICA HAD ONE TELEPHONE SYSTEM. WE USE TO CALL IT MA BELL.

BELL TELEPHONE SYSTEM

GLASS CANDY CONTAINERS

VERY SWEET TASTING CANDY

3½"

SHAPED LIKE CARS, TRAINS, BOATS ETC. THESE SMALL CONTAINERS CONTAINED TINY BEADS OF MULTI COLORED CANDIES.

USUALLY ONE PHONE PER HOUSEHOLD LOCATED IN HALLWAY OR ENTRY WAY

TELEPHONE STAND WITH PHONE

CRYING ROOM
IN MOVIE THEATERS

WAH WAH WAH WAH WAH

EXIT

The crying room was used for nursing mothers and crying kids. The room was sound proof. With a speaker and window to hear and watch the movie.

HEY! LETS GET THE SHOW ON THE ROAD.

WE HAVENT GOT ALL NIGHT!

NOT AGAIN

HOLD YOUR HORSES!

FLAP FLAP FLAP

KEEP OUT

ROOM WAS FILLED WITH THICK CIGARETTE SMOKE

WHO BAT'S FIRST

I'M UP!

4. 3. 2. 1.

EACH KID PLACED ONE HAND AT A TIME UP THE BAT HANDLE. FIRST ONE TO THE TOP CUPPED THE BAT HANDLE WITH HAND AND WOULD GO TO THE PLATE.

The Projection Room
AT TIMES THE FILM WOULD BREAK OFF CAUSING A 5-10 MINUTE DELAY OF THE FILM. A FLAPPING SOUND COULD BE HEARD FROM THE ROOM. THE SCREEN WENT TOTALY WHITE.

The Pea shooter

(BLOW GUN)

GETTING CAUGHT WAS NO FUN!

READY...AIM...BLOW!
This toy was a trouble maker BUT fun. Parents disliked the Pea Shooter

AMMUNITION

PLASTIC TUBE — 9"

INSERT BEAN AND BLOW

DRIED PEAS
MORE POPULAR IN EARLIER YEARS

SMALL WHITE BEANS
THESE WERE THE BEST

GREEN SPLIT PEAS
NOT AS GOOD BUT YOU GOT MORE AMO FOR THE BUCK.

OTHER PROJECTILES WERE: WADDED CANDY & GUM WRAPPERS

KNIFE SHARPENER

GRINDING WHEEL

FILES RAG

BELL

OIL

Walking down the street with his wheel cart and leather apron the man sharpend household knives and lawn mower blades

AS WHEEL TURNED BELL WENT DING...DING ...DING...

PRODUCE TRUCK

CANVAS ROLLED DOWN ON SIDES

FARM FRESH

About twice a week the Produce truck made its route through the neighborhood selling fresh produce straight from the farm.

Love Chain

Made with empty gum wrappers

The length of the chain was determined on the height of the boy you liked.

GLUED OR TAPED AT THE ENDS

7 STEPS FOR MAKING A LOVE CHAIN

① ② ③ ④ ⑤ ⑥ ⑦

FINISHED PIECE OF CHAIN

BUNNY BAG
A SMALL CLOTH SACK FILLED WITH WHITE POWDER USED FOR COVERING SCUFF MARKS

WHITE BUCKS
A white suede shoe popular with both boys and girls.

ZOOM!

BUSTER BROWN SHOES
I'M BUSTER BROWN, I LIVE IN A SHOE, THATS MY DOG, TIGE HE LIVES THERE TOO!

THE M-80 FIRE CRACKER
USE EMPTY CAN — PUNCH HOLE IN LID — INSERT M-80 IN HOLE MAKE SURE IT'S A SNUG FIT — PLACE CAN IN A PAN OF WATER — LIGHT M-80 AND RUN. UP, UP and away!

And Then Came...

PUBLISHER'S NOTE

I've known "Denny" for forty-eight years. His creative, humorous, kind and gentle nature has always been his way. He sees and then illustrates life situations in his own unique way which the rest of us often delightedly or sometimes uncomfortably recognize in ourselves. The laughter and fun times with Denny always come forth as he brings out humor and irony in every day life. With all that he accomplishes he still tends to be modest in his perception of these very special skills. His generosity toward everyone is shown in the relationships he has with his longtime neighbors and friends who regularly hang out on his front porch throughout the year, especially in the summertime. He's always had a special place in his heart for his beloved mother, Hilma, and his labrador, Sean, both deceased, who are often subtly included in much of his work.

An illustrator-cartoonist for more than four decades, Dennis Adler grew up in Portland, Oregon, as an only child, having a very large extended family of aunts, uncles, and cousins in Oregon and Washington. In addition to his ongoing artistic endeavors, for his own enjoyment and that of others, he occasionally plays his bongo drums at Moon and Sixpence, a local British pub. In this book, *Wax Lips and White Bucks*, he reflects on his, his family's, and my own memories of life growing up in the Forties, Fifties, and even the Sixties.

Thank you for choosing this book and sharing the essence of its contents. We have found that the subject matter herein has been a profound stimulus for laughter, conversation and discussion of fond memories for most adults of all ages, as well as for sharing "What we did" with younger generations. I hope you have enjoyed your remembrances through these pages.

Eric L. Burbano
STOOP ID Publications LLC

THAT'S ME, BOTTOM ROW 6TH FROM LEFT

About the Author:
Born and raised in Portland, Oregon, Dennis Adler has been a cartoonist and illustrator for forty-five years. He attended the Museum Art School (now Pacific Northwest College of Art) and Portland State University.

Credits
Books:
Bible Stories, Heaven and Mirth series/Cook Communications
High Country Prints Book/ Touchstone Press
Barnaby Frost/Tyndale House Publications
Poof The Magic Mountain/ Mitchel Davis & Drew

Greeting Cards:
Rabbi Rosenberg/© Rabbi Rosenberg Cards
Score Cards/Adler-Ring Production
What A Sport/Carol Wilson Fine Arts
Boomer Blues/ Boomer Blues Productions
Christmas Cards/West Graphics, San Francisco, CA

Posters:
Fund For Animals/ Cleveland Amory, New York, NY
Portland Poster/Meier & Frank Co.
First Presbyterian Church of Portland/ Adler Production
Cartoons: Reminisce Magazine (Does Anyone Remember?)
Readers Digest Association,Inc
"The New Breed"/King Features Syndication, New York

Photo courtesy Maryanne Caruthers

I hope you have enjoyed
this book about the things I
remember growing up as a kid in the
late 40s and early 50s. For some kids
these were the most wonderful and simple
times. We played street games 'till
dusk. Mom was always home. Doors were
never locked and on Halloween we went
trick or treating for blocks without
a parent escort.